CONTENTS

GRADE 1

ISBN: 978-1-927042-10-6

Comparing, Ordering, and Sequencing

Write the letters in the ☐ .

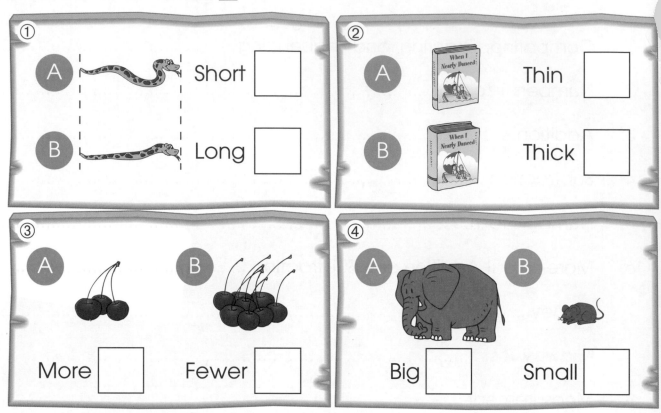

① A 🐍 Short ☐
  B 🐍 Long ☐

② A 📕 Thin ☐
  B 📗 Thick ☐

③ A 🍒 B 🍒 More ☐ Fewer ☐

④ A 🐘 B 🐭 Big ☐ Small ☐

Draw the pictures.

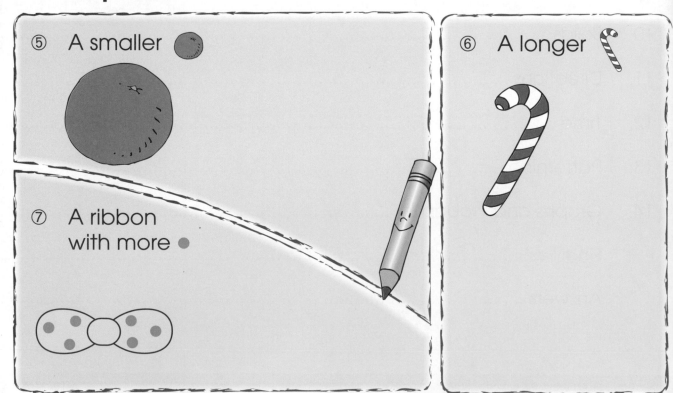

⑤ A smaller ●

⑥ A longer 🍬

⑦ A ribbon with more ●

Canadian Curriculum MathSmart (Grade 1)   ISBN: 978-1-927042-10-6

Put the things in order. Number them 1, 2, 3.

⑧ From short to long

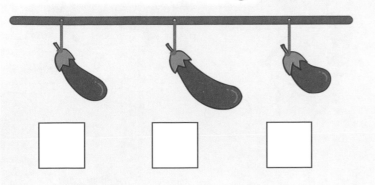

From big to small

2   1   3

This star is bigger than the other two.

⑨ From narrow to wide

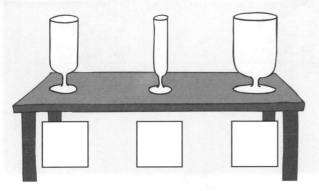

⑩ From thin to thick

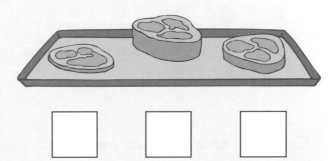

Check ✔ the correct order and put a cross ✘ for the wrong one.

⑪

⑫

ISBN: 978-1-927042-10-6

Put the pictures in order. Number them 1, 2, 3.

⑬

⑭

Circle ○ the correct answers.

⑮ 2   3   4 [cart] are empty.

⑯ [basketball] [bat] [girl] is in the 2nd [cart] .

⑰ [basketball] [girl] [bat] is in the 4th [cart] .

⑱ [teddy bear] is in the   1st   6th   2nd [cart] .

⑲ There are   5   6   7 [cart] .

> → [apple] [pear] [pear] [grapes] [banana] [cherry]
> The **2nd** and the **3rd** are pears. There are 2 pears.

Canadian Curriculum MathSmart (Grade 1)   ISBN: 978-1-927042-10-6

Look at the picture. Answer the questions.

⑳ Who is the 6th runner? _____

㉑ What is the position of Peter? _____

㉒ How many boys are there between the 2nd and the 6th boy? _____ boys

ACTIVITY

Match the people with their ✋. Write the letters.

ISBN: 978-1-927042-10-6

Numbers 1 to 20

Count and write the numbers.

Hello. My name is Jill. Can you help me count the cards?

Numbers 1 to 10

• 1	• • 2	•• • 3	•• •• 4
•• •• • 5	••• ••• 6	•• • •• 7
••• ••• •• 8	••• ••• ••• 9	••• ••• ••• 10

①

②

③

④

Write the numbers in words.

⑤   **6** _____   **3** _____

5 _____   **8** _____

Canadian Curriculum MathSmart (Grade 1)
ISBN: 978-1-927042-10-6

Count and write the numbers.

⑥

⑦

⑧

⑨

To count more easily, circle every 10 items first.

Count On
Small → Large
e.g.   1, 2, 3, 4, 5...
Count Back
Large → Small
e.g.   20, 19, 18, 17...

Decide whether the question is a "count-on" or "count-back" problem first. Then write the numbers.

Write the missing numbers.

⑩   3   4   [ ]   6   [ ]

⑪   9   10   [ ]   [ ]   13

⑫   10   9   [ ]   7   [ ]

⑬   15   [ ]   17   [ ]   19

⑭   13   [ ]   [ ]   16   17

⑮   16   15   [ ]   13   [ ]

⑯   11   [ ]   9   [ ]   7

ISBN: 978-1-927042-10-6

2

Look at each pair of bubbles. Colour the smaller number.

⑰

11 8   9 4   5 13

12 6   7 15

16 3   10 12

Count and colour the bones.

Colour the even numbers red and the odd numbers yellow.

⑱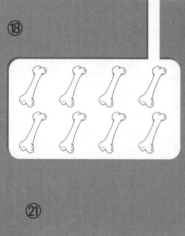

⑲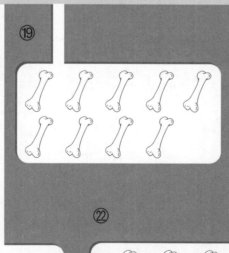

⑳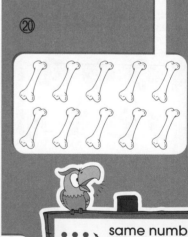

㉑

㉒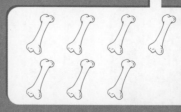

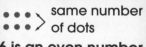

• • • • ⟩ same number of dots
• • • •
6 is an even number.

• • • ⟩ not the same
• •
5 is an odd number.

Canadian Curriculum MathSmart [Grade 1]   ISBN: 978-1-927042-10-6

Read what the children say. Colour their gifts.

The number of my gift is 1 more than 9. Colour it yellow.

The number of my gift is 2 more than 11. Colour it green.

The number of my gift is 1 less than 17. Colour it red.

| 5 more than 7 |
| Count on |
| 7 8 9 10 11 12 |
| 5 less than 12 |
| Count back |
| 7 8 9 10 11 12 |

㉓

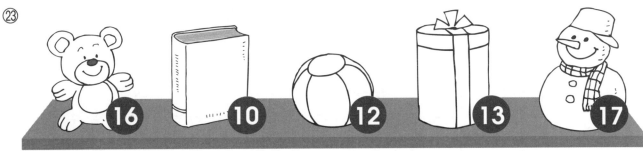

16   10   12   13   17

A C T I V I T Y

Colour the lily pads with odd numbers to help Little Frog cross the river.

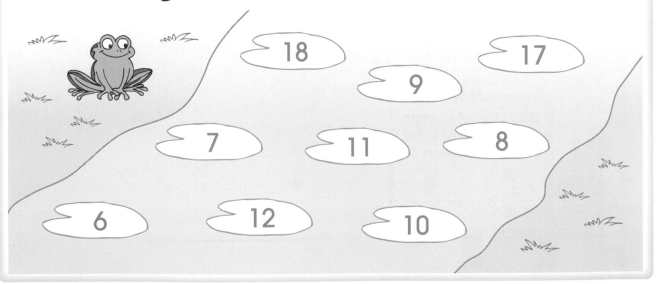

18   17
    9
7   11   8
6   12   10

ISBN: 978-1-927042-10-6

3 Addition

Count and write the numbers.

①

□ and □ makes □ .

□ + □ = □

"And" means plus. Join the groups to find the total, e.g.

1 and 2 makes 3.
1 + 2 = 3

②

□ and □ makes □ .

□ + □ = □

③

□
+ □
―――
□

④ □
+ □
―――
□
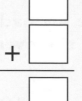

⑤ □
□
+ □
―――

Don't forget to align the numbers for vertical addition.

```
  2
+ 3    ✗
  5
```
```
  2
+ 3    ✓
  5
```

ISBN: 978-1-927042-10-6

Help Joe count the little creatures. Write the numbers in the ☐.

$$8 \quad + \quad 5 \quad = \quad 10 \quad + \quad 3 \quad = \quad 13$$

⑥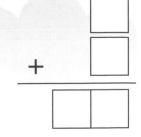

$$7 \quad + \quad \boxed{} \quad = \quad \boxed{}$$

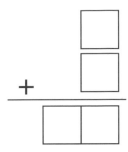

$$\boxed{} + \boxed{} \atop \boxed{}\boxed{}$$

⑦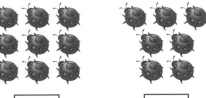

$$\boxed{} \quad + \quad \boxed{} \quad = \quad \boxed{}$$

$$\boxed{} + \boxed{} \atop \boxed{}\boxed{}$$

> Use the worms to help you count and find the answers.

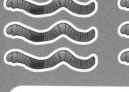
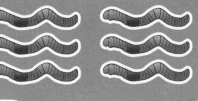

⑧
$$\begin{array}{r} 4 \\ + \ 1 \\ \hline \boxed{} \end{array}$$

⑨
$$\begin{array}{r} 3 \\ + \ 5 \\ \hline \boxed{} \end{array}$$

⑩
$$\begin{array}{r} 9 \\ + \ 2 \\ \hline \boxed{}\boxed{} \end{array}$$

⑪
$$\begin{array}{r} 7 \\ + \ 8 \\ \hline \boxed{}\boxed{} \end{array}$$

⑫ $6 + 4 = \boxed{}$

⑬ $4 + 8 = \boxed{}$

ISBN: 978-1-927042-10-6

Write the numbers.

Count the food and drinks for the party.

⑭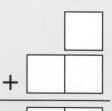

☐ + ☐ = ☐

⑮ ☐ + ☐ = ☐

Read what Mark and Jill say. Write the numbers.

I have 2 POP .
He has 3 POP .
We have
2 + 3 = ☐5☐ POP .

I have 3 POP .
She has 2 POP .
We have
3 + 2 = ☐5☐ POP .

Even if the order of addition changes, the answer is the same.
e.g.
♥ + ♥♥ = ♥♥ + ♥

☐2☐ + ☐3☐ = ☐3☐ + ☐2☐

⑯ 4 + 8 = ☐ + 4   ⑰ 1 + ☐ = 9 + 1

⑱ ☐ + 1 = 1 + 11   ⑲ 12 + 6 = 6 + ☐

ISBN: 978-1-927042-10-6

Fill in the boxes.

⑳ There are 2 and 7 on the farm. There are ☐ animals in all.

㉑ Peter picks 8 🍎 and Mary picks 6 🍎. They pick ☐ apples in all.

㉒ There are 12 🐦 in the tree. If 4 more 🐦 join the group, there will be ☐ birds in the tree.

㉓ Alexander has 5 🟠. If his mother gives him 7 more, he will have ☐ oranges in all.

ACTIVITY

Who has caught more fish?

I've caught 14 sunfish and 4 big bass.

I've caught 9 sunfish and 8 bass.

Tom

Ann

_____ has caught more fish.

ISBN: 978-1-927042-10-6

4 Subtraction

Cross out ✗ the bones. Then write how many bones are left.

① Cross out 7.

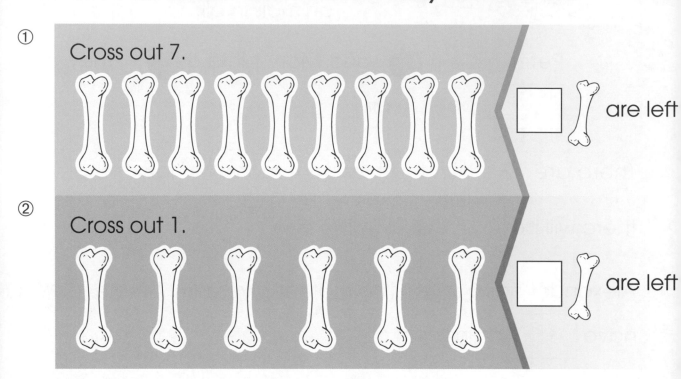

are left

② Cross out 1.

are left

Count and write the numbers.

③

☐ take away ☐ leaves ☐ .

☐ − ☐ = ☐

> "Take away" means minus.
> e.g.
> "3 take away 1 leaves 2" can be written as 3 − 1 = 2.

④

☐ minus ☐ equals ☐ .

☐ − ☐ = ☐

Canadian Curriculum MathSmart (Grade 1)

ISBN: 978-1-927042-10-6

How many fish are left?

⑤

$$8 - 5 = \boxed{}$$

⑥

$$\boxed{} - \boxed{} = \boxed{}$$

Don't forget to align the numbers.

$$\begin{array}{r} 5 \\ - 2 \\ \hline 3 \end{array} \; \times \qquad \begin{array}{r} 5 \\ - 2 \\ \hline 3 \end{array} \; \checkmark$$

⑦
$$\begin{array}{r} \boxed{} \\ - \boxed{} \\ \hline \boxed{} \end{array}$$

⑧
$$\begin{array}{r} \boxed{} \\ - \boxed{} \\ \hline \boxed{} \end{array}$$
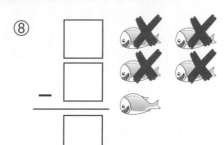

Do the subtraction.

⑨
$$\begin{array}{r} 3 \\ - 1 \\ \hline \boxed{} \end{array}$$

⑩
$$\begin{array}{r} 4 \\ - 2 \\ \hline \boxed{} \end{array}$$

⑪
$$\begin{array}{r} 7 \\ - 6 \\ \hline \boxed{} \end{array}$$

⑫
$$\begin{array}{r} 5 \\ - 2 \\ \hline \boxed{} \end{array}$$

⑬ $8 - 2 = \boxed{}$

⑭ $9 - 3 = \boxed{}$

⑮ $9 - 4 = \boxed{}$

⑯ $6 - 5 = \boxed{}$

ISBN: 978-1-927042-10-6

Do the subtraction.

Make use of 10 to do the subtraction.

e.g.

```
  1 3
-   6
```

Think:

13 = 10 + 3

```
  13
-  6
```

Subtract 6 from 10, and then add 3.

```
  1 3
-   6
    7
```

You can use counters to check the answers.
e.g.

```
  15
-  9
   6
```

⑰
```
  1 5
-   9
```

⑱
```
  1 2
-   3
```

⑲
```
  1 9
-   2
```

⑳
```
  1 8
-   7
```

㉑ 17 – 8 =

㉒ 12 – 6 =

㉓ 14 – 3 =

㉔ 18 – 9 =

㉕ 19 – 6 =

㉖ 11 – 8 =

㉗ 13 – 7 =

㉘ 16 – 5 =

㉙ 17 – 4 =

㉚ 15 – 7 =

Canadian Curriculum MathSmart (Grade 1)   ISBN: 978-1-927042-10-6

Write the numbers.

③① Mary makes 9  . If 3 are

taken away, there are ☐ left.

③② There are 14 . If 6 are for boys, ☐ are for girls.

③③ There are 15 and 8 at the party. The number of

is ☐ more than .

③④ Ann makes 19 . If she

gives 8 to her friends,

she has ☐ left.

 **A C T I V I T Y**

Solve the problem.

Aunt May has 3 plates. Each can hold 2 . If she puts her
on the plates, how many will be left on the tray?

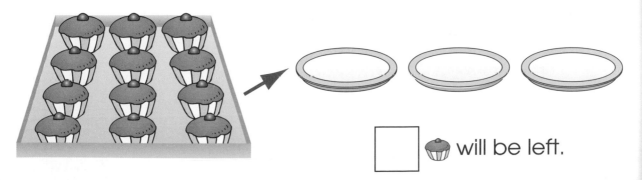

☐ will be left.

ISBN: 978-1-927042-10-6

Look at the lockers. Do the questions.

① Write the missing numbers.

② has a 🐭 on her locker door. Her locker number is

[   ] .

③ has a 🐰 on his locker door. His locker number is

[   ] .

④ Write the numbers of the opened lockers from small to large:

[   ] , [   ] , 46, 51, [   ]

Fill in the missing numbers.

⑤
a. 76, [ ] , 78, [ ] , [ ] , [ ]
b. 94, [ ] , [ ] , [ ] , 98, [ ]

⑥
a. 65, [ ] , [ ] , 62, [ ] ,
b. [ ] , 71, 70, [ ] , [ ] , [ ] ,

Count and write the numbers.

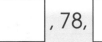
The digit in the ones place is any number less than ten, e.g.

23 =

2 tens 3 ones

⑦
[2] tens [4] ones = [24]

⑧
[ ] tens [ ] ones = [ ]

⑨
[ ] tens [ ] ones = [ ]

⑩
[ ] tens [ ] ones = [ ]

ISBN: 978-1-927042-10-6

Fill in the blanks.

⑪ 4 tens 1 one = _____

⑫ 9 tens 3 ones = _____

⑬ 8 tens = _____

⑭ 6 tens = _____

⑮ _____ tens 2 ones = 52

⑯ _____ tens 6 ones = 66

⑰ 1 ten _____ ones = 19

⑱ _____ ones = 3

Circle ◯ the better estimates. Then count and write the numbers.

⑲

more than 30

fewer than 30

⑳
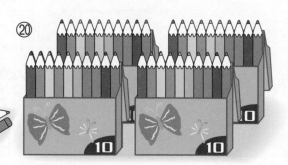

more than 50

fewer than 50

Circle ◯ the things in groups of 10. Count and write the numbers.

㉑
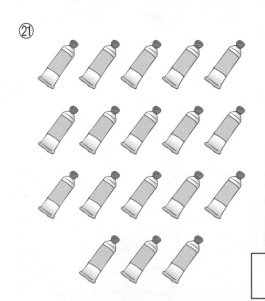

㉒
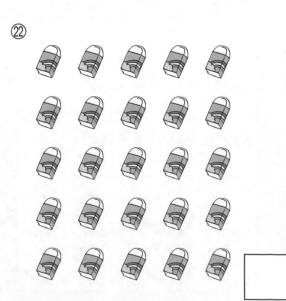

ISBN: 978-1-927042-10-6

Count the **by 5's and 10's.**
Write the numbers.

Read this first!

e.g.   Count by 5's: 5 $\xrightarrow{+5}$ 10 $\xrightarrow{+5}$ 15 $\xrightarrow{+5}$ 20 $\xrightarrow{+5}$ ...

Count by 10's: 10 $\xrightarrow{+10}$ 20 $\xrightarrow{+10}$ 30 $\xrightarrow{+10}$ 40 $\xrightarrow{+10}$ ...

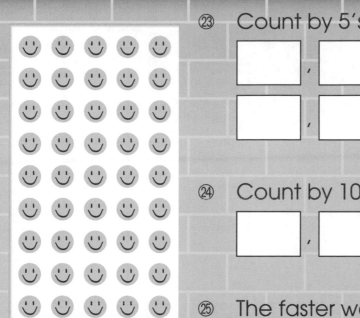

㉓ Count by 5's.

[ ] , [ ] , [ ] , [ ] , [ ] ,

[ ] , [ ] , [ ] , [ ] , [ ]

㉔ Count by 10's.

[ ] , [ ] , [ ] , [ ] , [ ]

㉕ The faster way to count is by [ ]'s.

A C T I V I T Y

Count by 2's. Colour the path and circle ◯ the thing that Dan wants.

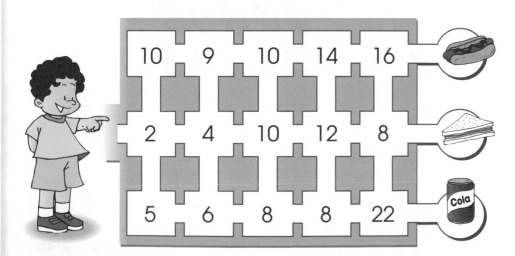

10	9	10	14	16
2	4	10	12	8
5	6	8	8	22

Count by 2's:

2 $\xrightarrow{+2}$ 4 $\xrightarrow{+2}$ 6

$\xrightarrow{+2}$ 8 $\xrightarrow{+2}$ 10

$\xrightarrow{+2}$ ...

ISBN: 978-1-927042-10-6

6 More about Addition and Subtraction

Look at the numbers on the flowers. Complete the number sentences.

①
3   2   5

$2 + 3 = \underline{}$

$3 + 2 = \underline{}$

$5 - 3 = \underline{}$

$5 - \underline{} = 3$

②
4   9   13

$4 + 9 = \underline{}$

$9 + 4 = \underline{}$

$13 - 4 = \underline{}$

$13 - \underline{} = 4$

③ **9   7   16**

$7 + 9 = \underline{}$

$9 + 7 = \underline{}$

$16 - 9 = \underline{}$

$16 - \underline{} = 9$

Write an addition sentence and a subtraction sentence for each group of pictures.

④

☐ + ☐ = ☐

☐ − ☐ = ☐

⑤

☐ + ☐ = ☐

☐ − ☐ = ☐

Find the answers.

Super!

⑥ 5
  + 2
  ☐

⑦ 6
  − 1
  ☐

⑧ 4
  + 3
  ☐

⑨ 9
  − 4
  ☐

⑩ 1 4
  −   2
  ☐

⑪   7
  + 8
  ☐

⑫ 1 8
  −   9
  ☐

⑬   9
  + 2
  ☐

⑭ 1 3
  −   5
  ☐

⑮ 1 7
  + 1
  ☐

Well done!

⑯ 7 − 6 = ☐

⑰ 2 + 6 = ☐

⑱ 12 + 3 = ☐

⑲ 16 − 3 = ☐

⑳ 8 + 8 = ☐

㉑ 14 − 5 = ☐

㉒ 9 + 1 = ☐

㉓ 5 + 7 = ☐

㉔ 11 − 3 = ☐

㉕ 10 − 4 = ☐

Name: **Bill**

Grade: *1*

> When you add or subtract, don't forget to align the numbers.
> e.g.   9   15
>   + 6   − 6
>   15 ←align   9 ←align

ISBN: 978-1-927042-10-6

Read what the children say. Fill in the boxes.

㉖   I have 8 . My brother has 4 . How many do we have in all?

☐ + ☐ = ☐

We have ☐ in all.

☐
+ ☐
─────
☐

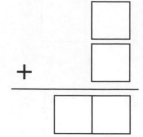

㉗  My mother made 17 . My sister and I ate 8 . How many are left?

☐ − ☐ = ☐

☐ are left.

☐
− ☐
─────
☐

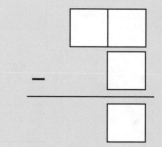

㉘   There are 11 in the bag. If I take 7 , how many will be left in the bag?

☐ − ☐ = ☐

☐ will be left in the bag.

☐
− ☐
─────
☐

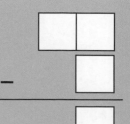

Canadian Curriculum MathSmart (Grade 1)   ISBN: 978-1-927042-10-6

Circle ◯ the correct signs. Then solve the problems.

㉙ There are 8 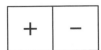 and 5 on a tray. How many food items are there?

+	−

☐ food items

㉚ A group has 13 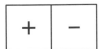 and 6 . How many more than are there?

+	−

☐ more

A C T I V I T Y

Write the missing numbers.

① 11 − ☐ = 7   ② 5 + ☐ = 8

③ 15 − ☐ = 6   ④ 1 + ☐ = 11

⑤ ☐ − 7 = 5   ⑥ ☐ + 9 = 14

3

5   10   9   4   12

ISBN: 978-1-927042-10-6

Money

Penny	1¢
Nickel	5¢
Dime	10¢
Quarter	25¢
Loonie	$1
Toonie	$2

Write the names and values of the coins.

① _____ , $ ☐

② _____ , $ ☐

③ _____ , ☐ ¢

④ _____ , ☐ ¢

⑤ _____ , ☐ ¢

⑥ _____ , ☐ ¢

Count and write the numbers.

⑦ ☐ pennies

☐ nickels

☐ dimes

☐ quarters

☐ loonies

☐ toonies

Canadian Curriculum MathSmart (Grade 1)   ISBN: 978-1-927042-10-6

Circle ◯ the coin that has the greatest value in each group.

Check ✔ the coins to match the value of the coin on the left.

Write how much each girl has. Then answer the questions.

⑯

[ ] ¢

⑰

[ ] ¢

⑱

[ ] ¢

⑲

[ ] ¢

⑳ Circle ◯ the girl who has the least money.

㉑ Write the numbers 1– 4 in the ☐ . Start with the girl who has the most money.

 [ ]  [ ]  [ ]  [ ]

Canadian Curriculum MathSmart (Grade 1) ISBN: 978-1-927042-10-6

Look at the prices of the toys. Solve the problems.

㉒ How much do a and a  cost?

[ ] + [ ] = [ ]

They cost [ ] ¢.

㉓ Leo has 10¢. If he buys a 🚗, how much will be left?

[ ] – [ ] = [ ]

[ ] ¢ will be left.

SALE

9¢

4¢

2¢

 A C T I V I T Y

John and Jill share the coins equally. How many coins does each get? How much does each have?

① Each gets [ ] coins.

② Each has [ ] ¢.

ISBN: 978-1-927042-10-6

Canadian Curriculum MathSmart (Grade 1)

Midway Test

Put the things in order. Number them 1, 2, 3. (6 marks)

① From big to small

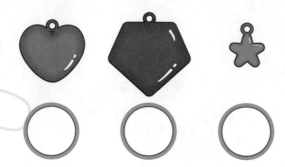

② From wide to narrow

Write the ordinal numbers to show the order of the pictures. Then fill in the blanks. (12 marks)

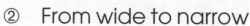

Steps to make a necklace for EMILY

③

1st

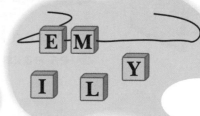

④ **M** is the _____ bead.

⑤ There are _____ beads between the 2nd and the 5th bead.

Count and write the number of animals. Then write the numbers in words. (8 marks)

a.	Sheep	
b.	Cow	

Circle ◯ the animals in groups of 10. Write the numbers. (4 marks)

⑦

⑧

Write the numbers on the eggs. (6 marks)

⑨ 5   6   ___   ___   9   ___

⑩ ___   ___   27   26   ___   24

⑪ ___   78   ___   ___   81   82

ISBN: 978-1-927042-10-6

Midway Test

Continue the patterns. Write the numbers. (6 marks)

⑫

Count by _____'s.

⑬

Count by _____'s.

⑭

Count by _____'s.

Write the numbers in the boxes. (13 marks)

⑮ 1 more than 7 = ☐

⑯ 2 less than 5 = ☐

⑰ 4 less than 12 = ☐

⑱ 5 more than 9 = ☐

⑲ 38 = ☐ tens ☐ ones

⑳ ☐ = 5 tens 7 ones

㉑ 21 = 2 tens ☐ one

㉒ 94 = ☐ tens 4 ones

㉓ 9 = ☐ ones

㉔ 60 = ☐ tens

㉕ ☐ = 8 tens

㉖ ☐ = 6 ones

ISBN: 978-1-927042-10-6

Name the coins and write the values. (8 marks)

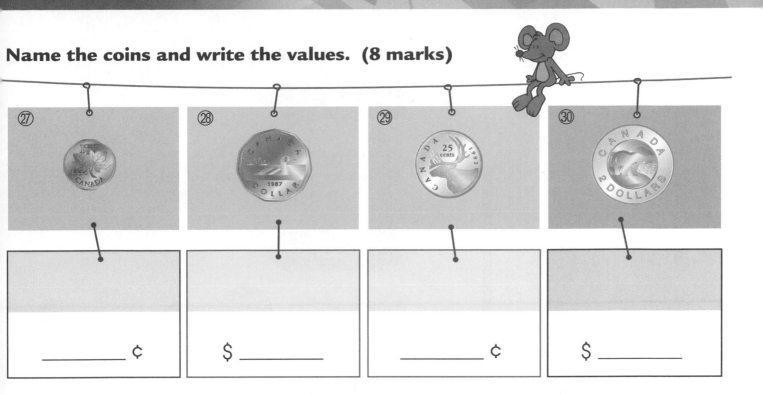

㉗ _____ ¢

㉘ $ _____

㉙ _____ ¢

㉚ $ _____

Write the amount of each group of coins. Then check ✔ the group with the greatest value. (6 marks)

㉛

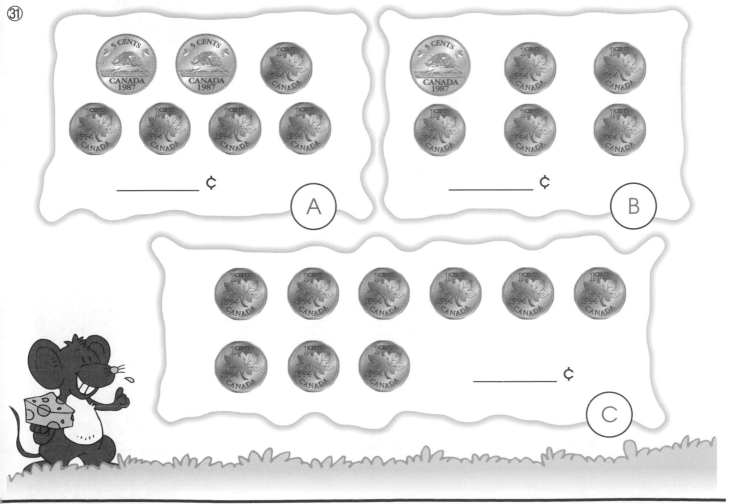

A _____ ¢

B _____ ¢

C _____ ¢

Midway Test

Check ✔ the coins to match the price of each thing. (6 marks)

Sale

Book 8¢

4¢

10¢ Puzzle

③② **A book**

③③ **A car**

③④ **A puzzle**

Find the answers. (10 marks)

③⑤
$$3 + 1 = \boxed{}$$

③⑥
$$8 - 6 = \boxed{}$$

③⑦
$$17 - 9 = \boxed{}$$

③⑧
$$7 + 8 = \boxed{}$$

③⑨ $6 + 2 = \boxed{}$

④⓪ $4 - 1 = \boxed{}$

④① $15 - 6 = \boxed{}$

④② $7 + 5 = \boxed{}$

④③ $13 - 8 = \boxed{}$

④④ $9 + 3 = \boxed{}$

ISBN: 978-1-927042-10-6

Solve the problems. (15 marks)

㊺ A costs 6¢. Ann has  .
If she buys a  , how much will
be left?

[ ] ¢

—
_____

㊻

_____

There are 7 in the vase. If May puts
6 more in the vase, how many will
there be?

[ ] 🌸

㊼ There are 14 and 9 in a box.
How many more than are
there in the box?

[ ] more

_____

Score

100

8 Measurement

Look at the picture. Help Ann do the job.

① Check ✔ the longest 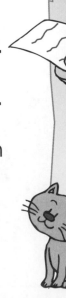 .

② Circle ◯ the smallest gift.

③ Put a cross ✘ on the tallest flower.

④ Colour the biggest picture blue.

⑤ Put the books in order from thin to thick.

◻ , ◻ , ◻

Canadian Curriculum MathSmart (Grade 1)   ISBN: 978-1-927042-10-6

**Measure the lengths of the objects with and ✏.
Write the numbers and answer the question.**

⑥

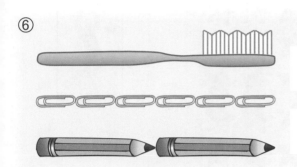

⑦

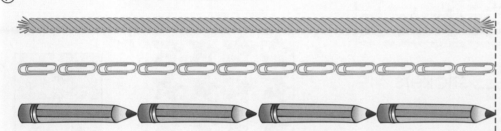

⑧ Check ✔ the longer unit.

A   B

Check ✔ the best unit for measuring each thing.

⑨

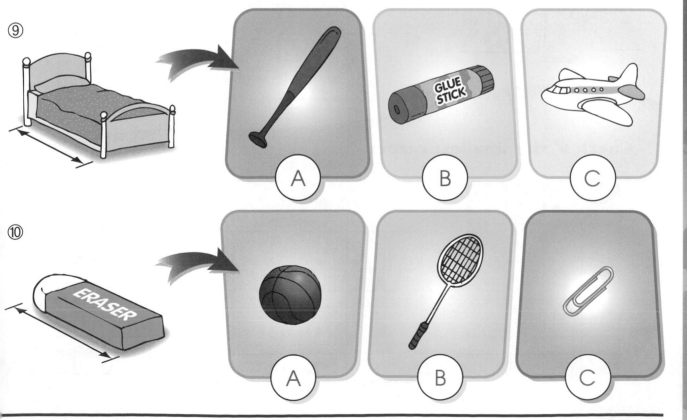

⑩

Find out how many stickers are needed to cover each card. Circle ⬭ the correct answer.

⑪ _____ stickers

⑫ _____ stickers

⑬ _____ stickers

Which card is the biggest?

⑭

Check ✔ the smallest carpet.

⑮

A   B   C

Colour the heavier thing in each pair.

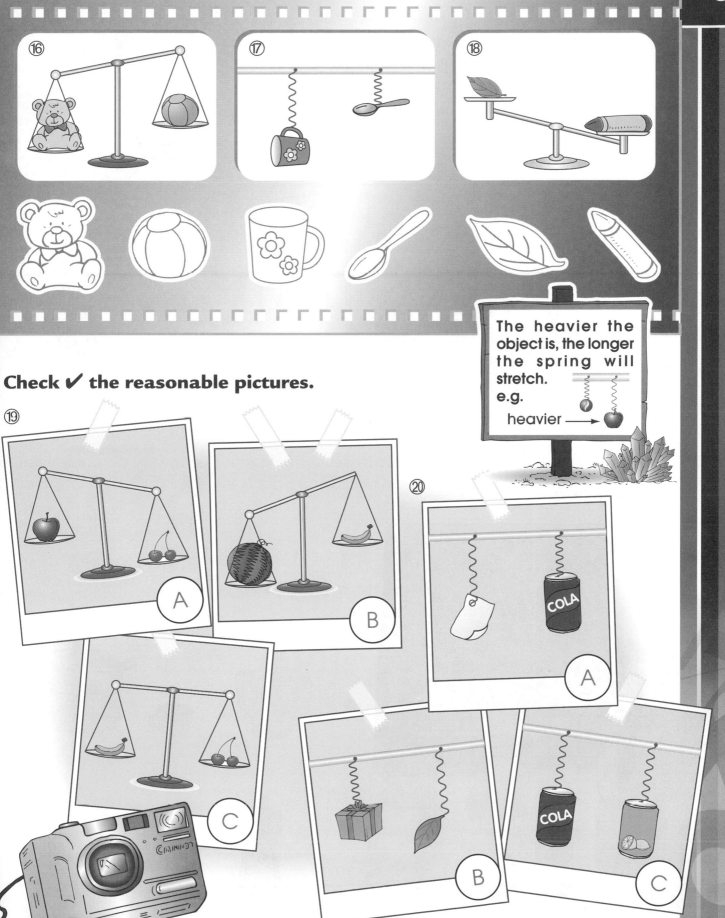

8

The heavier the object is, the longer the spring will stretch.

e.g.

heavier →

Check ✔ the reasonable pictures.

Help the children put the things in order. Start with the lightest. Number
them 1, 2, 3.

Circle ◯ the container
that holds the most in
each group.

 already placed

ISBN: 978-1-927042-10-6

Read what each container says.
Circle ◯ the best answer.

㉖ How many boxes of juice are needed to fill me up?

 1   10   90

㉗ I fill myself up with water 10 times. Which container can be filled up with all the water from me?

㉘ Which container holds about the same amount of water as me?

 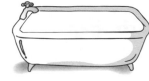

 Oops!

ACTIVITY

Draw a line to show how much water is in the can now.

I was full of water, but now I'm only half full.

ISBN: 978-1-927042-10-6

Trace the shapes. Then complete the names of the shapes.

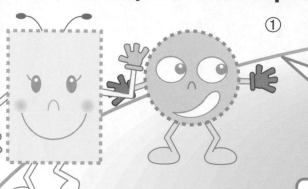

①

My name is C __ __ __ l __.
She is my friend. Her name is
R __ __ __ a __ __ __ e.

My friend, Tr __ __ __ __ l __,
is cute. People like to call me
S __ __ __ r __.

Pentagon

Hexagon

Oval

Count and write the number of each shape.

②

Circle   ____

Triangle   ____

Rectangle   ____

Square   ____

Hexagon   ____

Pentagon   ____

Oval   ____

Canadian Curriculum MathSmart (Grade 1)

ISBN: 978-1-927042-10-6

Join the dots in order. Then name the shapes and write the numbers.

③
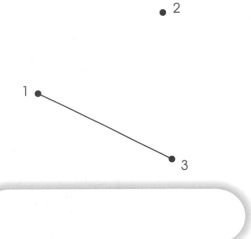

_____ sides

_____ corners

④

_____ sides

_____ corners

corner

side

A rectangle has 4 sides and 4 corners.

⑤

_____ sides

_____ corners

⑥

_____ sides

_____ corners

Draw the shapes.

⑦ A wider triangle

⑧ A taller triangle

Tall Wide

⑨ A wider, but shorter triangle

A symmetrical shape has two exactly matching sides.

Are these shapes symmetrical? Write "Yes" or "No".

Two sides of my face match exactly. My face is symmetrical.

⑩

⑪

⑫

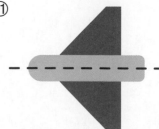

_____   _____   _____

Canadian Curriculum MathSmart (Grade 1)   ISBN: 978-1-927042-10-6

Draw a line to cut each shape into 2 matching parts.

⑬ ⑭ ⑮

⑯ ⑰

Symmetrical

Draw the missing part to make each picture symmetrical.

⑱ ⑲ ⑳

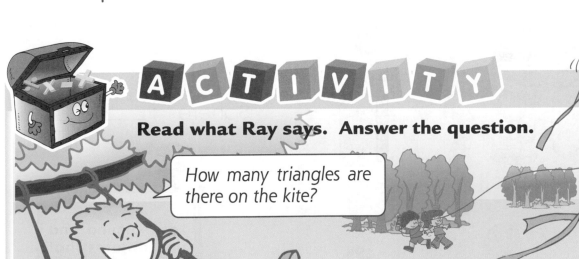

A C T I V I T Y

Read what Ray says. Answer the question.

How many triangles are there on the kite?

triangles

ISBN: 978-1-927042-10-6

Canadian Curriculum MathSmart (Grade 1)

10 **Solids**

Draw lines to match the solids with their names.

①

Prism •

Cylinder •

Cone •

Sphere •

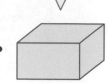 •

 •

•

•

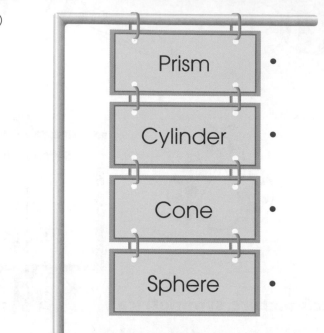

Look at the solids on the shelves. Write the letters.

② Cone : _____

Cylinder : _____

Prism : _____

Sphere : _____

Look around and find objects that match the things on the shelves.

ISBN: 978-1-927042-10-6

In each group, cross out ✗ the solid that does not belong. Then name the other solids.

③ Chocolate   Cola

④ Juice

⑤

⑥

Count and write the number of each solid.

⑦

: _____

: _____

: _____

: _____

ISBN: 978-1-927042-10-6

Colour the solids and circle ◯ the correct words.

⑧ Which solids can roll down a slope in a straight line?

⑨ Which solids can be stacked up?

⑩ Which solids have flat faces?

⑪ Which solids can slide?

Slide

Roll

⑫ Which solids can roll and slide?

Sphere   Prism

Cone   Cylinder

See how Andy traces the solids. Check ✔ the correct shapes.

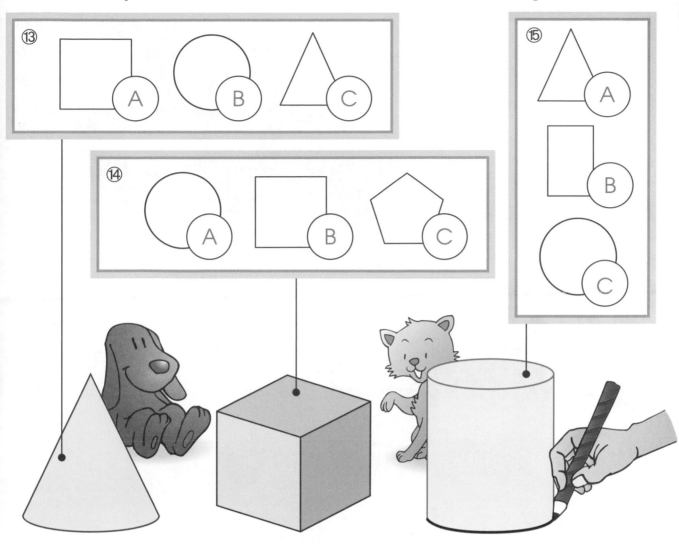

⑬ A   B   C

⑭ A   B   C

⑮ A   B   C

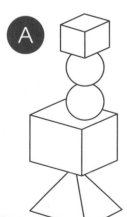

Colour the one that can stand.

A
B
C
D

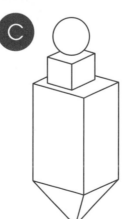
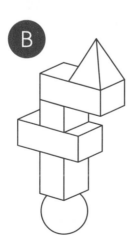
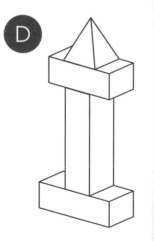

11 Directions

Look at the picture. Circle ○ the correct words.

①  is [behind   in front of] the .

② The 🦌 has a 🔔 in his [left   right] hand.

③ The 🎁 is [inside   outside] the 🛷 .

④ The ⭐ is jumping [over   under] the 🌙 .

⑤ The 🍪 is [behind   in front of] the
🛷 .

⑥ The 🎁 is [inside   outside] the .

Canadian Curriculum MathSmart (Grade 1)   ISBN: 978-1-927042-10-6

Look at the picture. Fill in the blanks with the given words.

in front of	behind	left	right
over	under	inside	outside

⑦ The  The 🐱 is on the _____ of 🧑 .

⑧ The 🪴 is on the _____ of the 🍷 .

⑨ The ✉️ is _____ the 🪑 .

⑩ The 🥤 is _____ the 🍷 .

⑪ The 🥤 is _____ the ✉️ .

⑫ The 🪑 is _____ 🧑 .

⑬ The 🪟 is _____ 🧑 .

⑭ The 🐦 is flying _____ the house.

Draw the things on the shelves.

⑮ There is a ⚽ on the left of the 🔺 .

⑯ There is an 🍎 under the 🚗 .

⑰ There is an 🍊 on the right of the 🏸 .

Read what Raymond and his dog say. Check ✔ the correct pictures.

⑱

I was on the left of my mom and behind my dad.

A   B   C

⑲

I slept under the table and inside the cage.

A   B   C

Canadian Curriculum MathSmart (Grade 1)   ISBN: 978-1-927042-10-6

Write a sentence to describe the position of each child.

Ⓠ20 Pat _____

_____ .

Ⓠ21 Annie _____ .

Ⓠ22 Michael _____ .

Ⓠ23 Jack _____ .

Ⓠ24 Tim _____ .

 A C T I V I T Y

Fill in the blanks.

① The is _____ the  .

② The has a  in his _____

hand.

ISBN: 978-1-927042-10-6

Spring, summer, fall, winter, spring, summer...

Name the seasons.

①

Put the seasons in order. Start with spring.

②

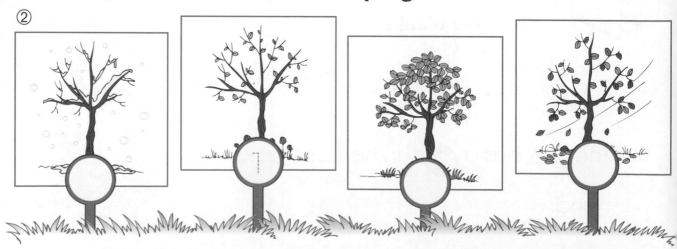

Look at the daily specials at Uncle Philip's restaurant. Answer the questions.

Daily Specials

Sunday

Monday

Tuesday

Wednesday

Thursday

Friday

Saturday

Cola

③ On which day is the hamburger on special offer?

_____

④ On which day is the pizza on special offer?

_____

⑤ Which day comes right after Monday?

_____

⑥ Which day comes right before Friday?

_____

⑦ Nicole buys a packet of fries on special offer. Which day is it?

_____

⑧ Tom likes sandwiches. Which day is Tom's favourite day?

_____

⑨ How many days are there in a week?

_____

⑩ How many days are there between Monday and Friday?

_____

Sunday is the first day of the week.

Saturday is the last day of the week.

Write the times.

The long hand is the minute hand. The short hand is the hour hand.

2:30

The hour hand points between 2 and 3. The minute hand points to 6.

Look at the clocks and circle ◯ the correct answers.

⑱ nearly 1:00

nearly 2:00

⑲ nearly 3:00

nearly 3:30

Canadian Curriculum MathSmart (Grade 1)   ISBN: 978-1-927042-10-6

Draw the clock hands.

⑳

A : I perform at 8:00.

B : I sing at 4:30.

C : I dance at 7:30.

ACTIVITY

Look at the time Tim arrived at each place. Draw a path from his house to the library.

Tim's house

Cinema

Museum

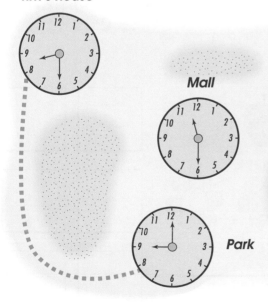

Mall

School

Park

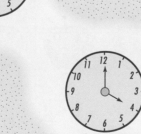

Library

ISBN: 978-1-927042-10-6

13 Patterning

Follow the patterns. Draw the missing pictures.

Continue the patterns.

ISBN: 978-1-927042-10-6

Colour the eggs. Answer the questions.

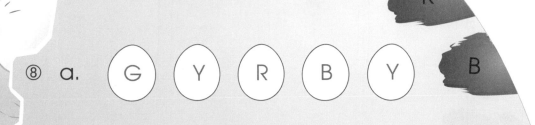

⑧ a. G Y R B Y B

b. Do the eggs follow a pattern? _____

⑨ a. B Y G B Y G B

b. Do the eggs follow a pattern? _____

Cross out ✗ the one that does not follow the pattern in each group.

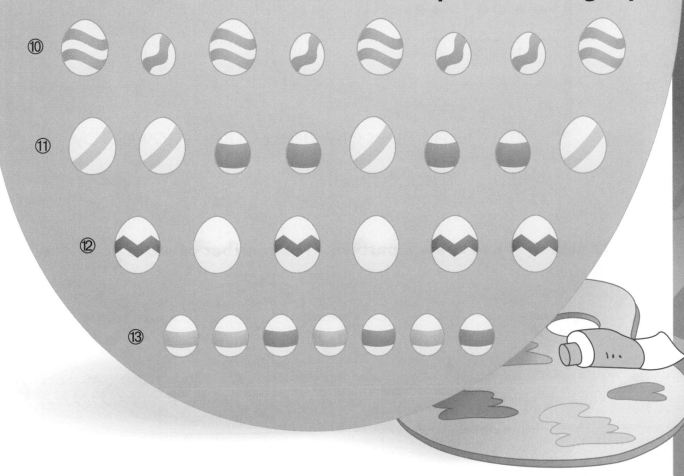

⑩

⑪

⑫

⑬

ISBN: 978-1-927042-10-6

13

Draw the next two pictures in the patterns. Then circle ◯ the correct answers and fill in the boxes.

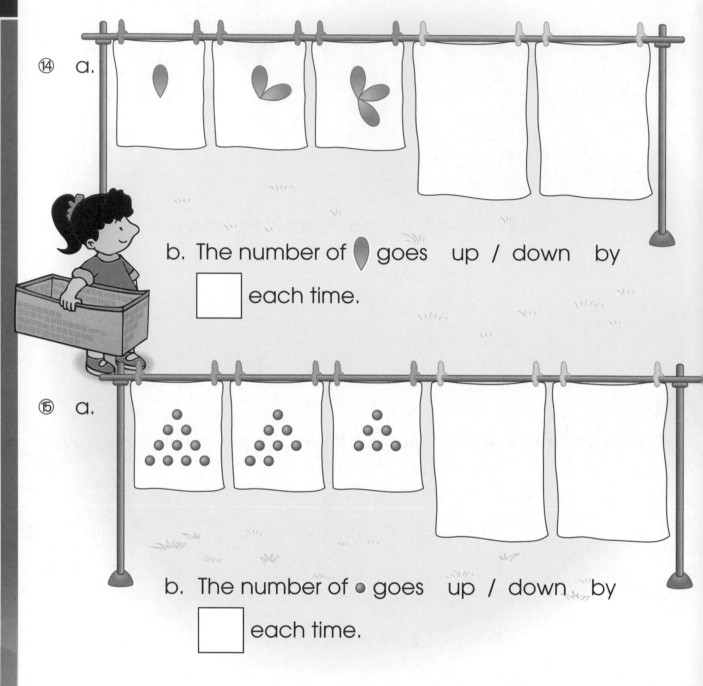

⑭ a.

b. The number of 🌱 goes   up / down   by [ ] each time.

⑮ a.

b. The number of ● goes   up / down   by [ ] each time.

Use 12 stars (☆) to draw a pattern. The number of stars goes down by 2 each time.

⑯

Write the numbers to complete the patterns. Then write the pattern rules.

⑰ 6, 8, 10, 12, ⬚ , ⬚ , ⬚

Pattern rule: _____

⑱ 15, 20, 25, 30, ⬚ , ⬚ , ⬚

Pattern rule: _____

⑲ 30, 40, 50, ⬚ , ⬚ , ⬚

Pattern rule: _____

2, 4, 6, 8, 10

+2 +2 +2 +2

Pattern rule:
+2 each time

A C T I V I T Y

Follow the pattern. Draw and colour the tiles.

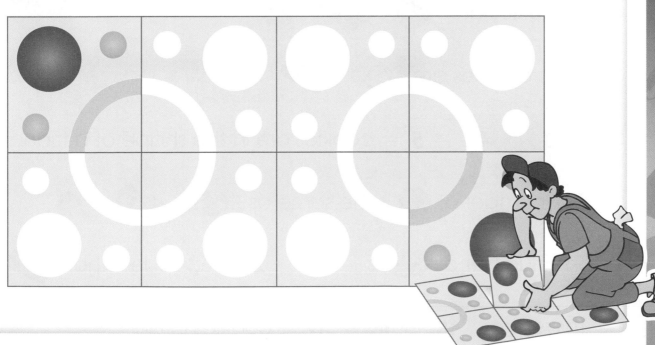

ISBN: 978-1-927042-10-6

Canadian Curriculum MathSmart (Grade 1)

Graphs and Probability

Ann's mother has made some cookies. Look at the graph and circle ◯ the correct answers.

Number of Cookies Made

① **3   4   5** cookies are 🍪 .

② 5 cookies are 🍪 🍪 🔺 .

③ Most cookies are 🍪 🍪 🔺 .

④ **3   4   5** cookies are in the shape of a triangle.

⑤ The number of 🍪 is the same as 🍪 🍪 🔺 .

⑥ The number of 🍪 is **1   2   3** less than 🍪 .

⑦ There are **15   16   17** cookies in all.

ISBN: 978-1-927042-10-6

Lucy has asked her friends about their favourite fruits. Look at her record. Colour the graph and answer the questions.

Colour the picture from the bottom of each column.

⑧

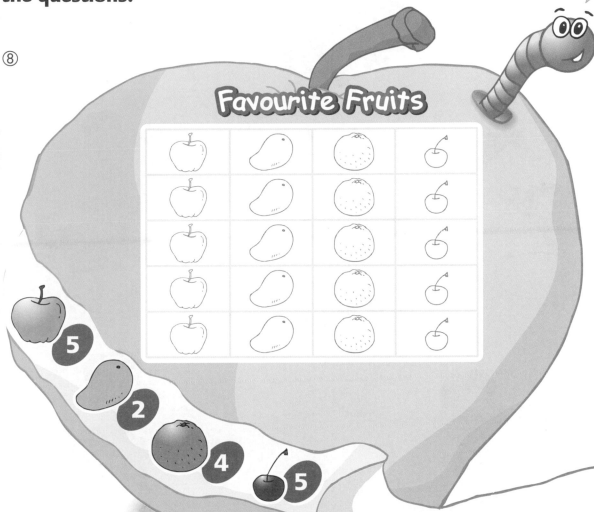

Favourite Fruits

⑨ How many children like ? _____

⑩ How many children like or ? _____

⑪ How many more children like than ? _____

⑫ How many children were asked? _____

⑬ How many kinds of fruits are there? _____

ISBN: 978-1-927042-10-6

14

Look at the pictures. Write "Yes" if Tom's dreams can come true. Write "No" if they cannot.

Lucy lets Tim pick a marble from her bag.
Help Tim circle ◯ the correct answers.

⑲ Will he get a ?

　　Yes　　No

⑳ Will he get a ?

　　Yes　　No

㉑ Will he get a ?

　　Yes　　No

ISBN: 978-1-927042-10-6

Write "often", "sometimes", or "never" to describe the chances. Then complete the sentences.

3 · 2 · 3 · 3 · 3

I'll pick a card without looking.

㉒

2 : _____

0 : _____

3 : _____

㉓ a. It _____ lands on yellow.

It _____ lands on blue.

It _____ lands on red.

b. It _____ lands on blue, but

it _____ lands on white. It

_____ lands on green.

A C T I V I T Y

Colour the spinner.

There are 2 sections on this spinner. The chances of landing on red and yellow are the same.

ISBN: 978-1-927042-10-6

Look at the pictures. Answer the questions. (12 marks)

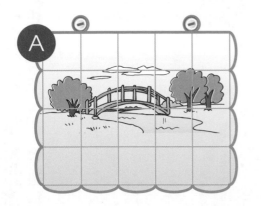

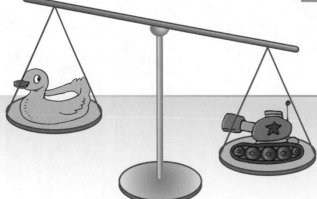

① is a bit [longer   shorter] than _____ .

② [A   B   C] is the largest picture. _____ ☐ are needed to cover it.

③ [A   B   C] is in the shape of a square.

④ The heaviest toy is [ ] .

Name the shapes. Then write the numbers. (20 marks)

⑤

_____

_____ sides

_____ corners

⑥

_____

_____ sides

_____ corners

⑦

_____

_____ sides

_____ corners

⑧

_____

_____ sides

_____ corners

Draw the lines of symmetry. (4 marks)

⑨

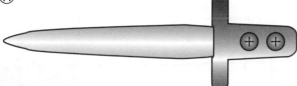

⑩

⑪

⑫

ISBN: 978-1-927042-10-6

Final Test

Name the solids. (4 marks)

⑬  _____

⑭ 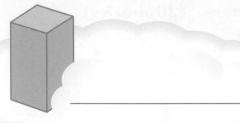 _____

⑮  _____

⑯ 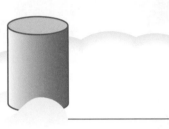 _____

Look at the solids in each group. Complete the sentences with the given words. (4 marks)

⑰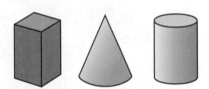

They have _____ .

⑱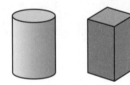

They can _____ .

> slide
> roll
> be stacked up
> flat faces

⑲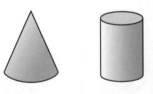

They can _____ and _____ .

ISBN: 978-1-927042-10-6

Look at the picture. Fill in the blanks with the given words. (8 marks)

inside / outside

over / under

in front of / behind

left / right

Doris

⑳ There is a Frisbee _____ Doris's head.

㉑ The bucket is _____ Doris.

㉒ Doris has a pair of sunglasses in her _____ hand.

㉓ The shells are _____ the bucket.

Find the answers. (8 marks)

㉔ a. Dan has 9 🐚 and Doris has 4. How many 🐚 do the children have in all?

[ ] 🐚

b. How many more 🐚 does Dan have than Doris?

[ ] more

㉕ a. There are 15 children on the beach. If there are 8 👦, how many 👧 are there?

b. If 6 more 👦 come to the beach, how many 👦 will there be?

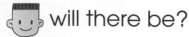

Final Test

Name the seasons. (4 marks)

Follow the patterns. Write the missing numbers or draw the missing shapes. (8 marks)

30. 3 4 5 3 4 5 ___ 4 ___ 3

31. ★ ♥ ★ ★ ___ ★ ★ ♥ ___ ★

ISBN: 978-1-927042-10-6

Write the numbers. (6 marks)

㉜ 2 more than 5 ______

㉝ 1 less than 40 ______

㉞ 3 tens 6 ones ______

㉟ 4 tens 5 ones ______

㊱ 8 tens ______

㊲ 2 tens ______

Follow the pattern to draw the clock hands and write the times. (4 marks)

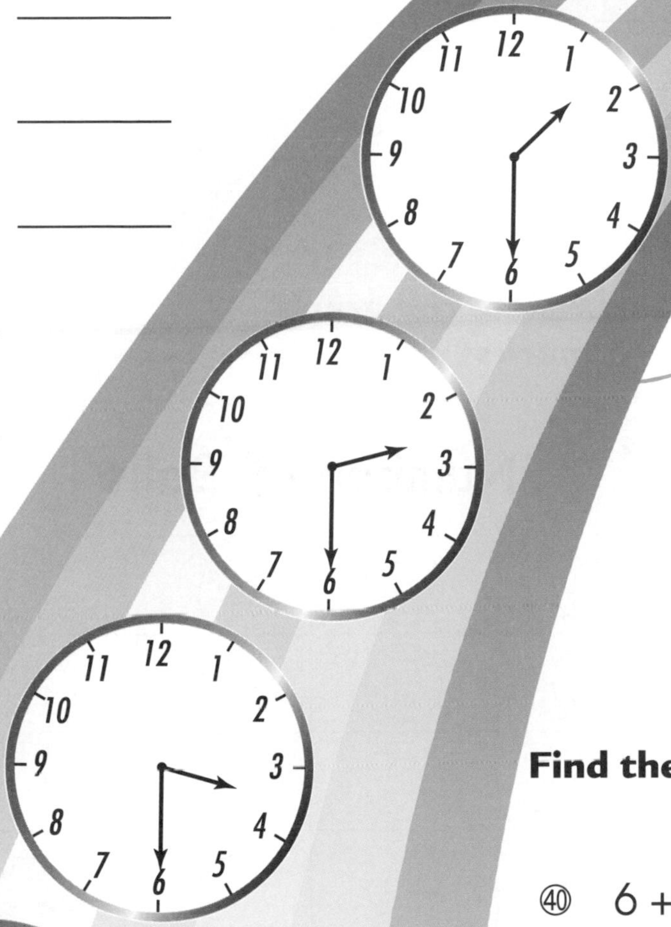

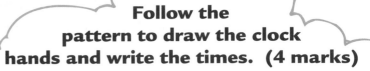

㊳

______

㊴

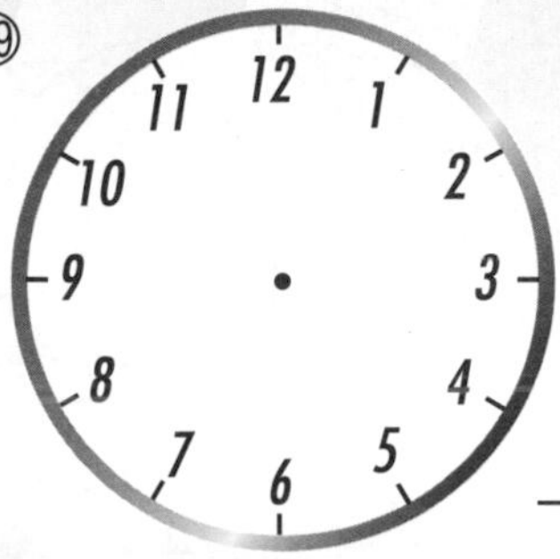

______

Find the answers. (7 marks)

㊵ 6 + 2 = ______

㊶ 7 + 4 = ______

㊷ 9 – 3 = ______

㊸ 16 – 8 = ______

㊹ 7 + 5 = ______

㊺ 11 – 9 = ______

㊻ 2 + 8 = ______

ISBN: 978-1-927042-10-6

Final Test

Sarah is going to pick a ball from the box without looking. Use "often", "sometimes", or "never" to describe the chances. (6 marks)

㊼ The chance of getting a

a. ⬤ _____

b. ⬤ _____

c. ⬤ _____

Colour the pictures to complete the graph. Answer the question. (5 marks)

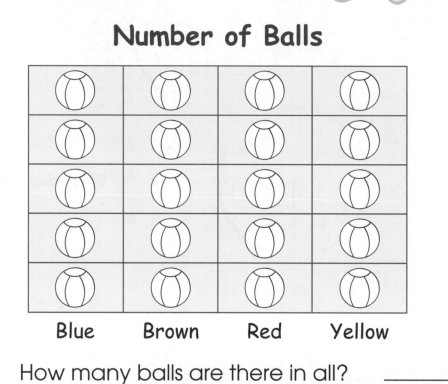

㊽

Number of Balls

Blue	Brown	Red	Yellow

㊾ How many balls are there in all? _____

ISBN: 978-1-927042-10-6

Score

100

1 Comparing, Ordering, and Sequencing

1. Short : B ; Long : A
2. Thin : A ; Thick : B
3. More : B ; Fewer : A
4. Big : A ; Small : B

5 - 7. (Suggested answers)

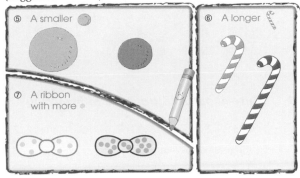

8. 2 ; 3 ; 1
9. 2 ; 1 ; 3
10. 1 ; 3 ; 2
11. ✗
12. ✔
13. 1 ; 3 ; 2
14. 1 ; 2 ; 3
15. 2
16.
17.
18. 1st
19. 6
20. Eric
21. The 7th
22. 3

Activity

A ; B ; C

2 Numbers 1 to 20

1. 5
2. 4
3. 7
4. 8
5. 6 : Six   3 : Three   5 : Five   8 : Eight   9 : Nine
6. 14
7. 16
8. 11
9. 12
10. 5 ; 7
11. 11 ; 12
12. 8 ; 6
13. 16 ; 18
14. 14 ; 15
15. 14 ; 12
16. 10 ; 8
17.

18. red
19. yellow
20. red
21. yellow
22. yellow
23.
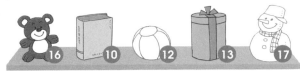

Activity

7 ; 11 ; 9 ; 17

3 Addition

1. 4 ; 2 ; 6 ; 4 ; 2 ; 6
2. 4 ; 5 ; 9 ; 4 ; 5 ; 9
3. 3 ; 3 ; 6
4. 3 ; 1 ; 4
5. 6 ; 3 ; 9
6. 6 ; 13 ; 7 + 6 = 13
7. 9 ; 7 ; 16 ; 9 + 7 = 16
8. 5
9. 8
10. 11
11. 15
12. 10
13. 12
14. 11 ; 1 ; 12 ; 11 + 1 = 12
15. 3 ; 12 ; 15 ; 3 + 12 = 15
16. 8
17. 9
18. 11
19. 12
20. 9
21. 14
22. 16
23. 12

Activity

Tom

4 Subtraction

1. 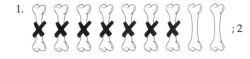 ; 2
2. ; 5
3. 5 ; 1 ; 4 ; 5 ; 1 ; 4
4. 8 ; 4 ; 4 ; 8 ; 4 ; 4
5. 3
6. 9 ; 2 ; 7
7. 6 ; 4 ; 2
8. 5 ; 4 ; 1
9. 2
10. 2
11. 1
12. 3
13. 6
14. 6

15. 5
16. 1
17. 6
18. 9
19. 17
20. 11
21. 9
22. 6
23. 11
24. 9
25. 13
26. 3
27. 6
28. 11
29. 13
30. 8
31. 6
32. 8
33. 7
34. 11

Activity

6

5 Numbers to 100

1.
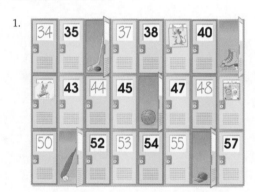

2. 39
3. 42
4. 36 ; 41 ; 56
5a. 77 ; 79 ; 80 ; 81
  b. 95 ; 96 ; 97 ; 99
6a. 64 ; 63 ; 61 ; 60
  b. 72 ; 69 ; 68 ; 67
7. 2 ; 4 ; 24
8. 3 ; 8 ; 38
9. 6 ; 3 ; 63
10. 7 ; 4 ; 74
11. 41
12. 93
13. 80
14. 60
15. 5
16. 6
17. 9
18. 3
19. more than 30 ; 33
20. fewer than 50 ; 42
21. 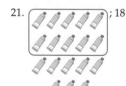 ; 18
22.  ; 25
23. 5 ; 10 ; 15 ; 20 ; 25 ; 30 ; 35 ; 40 ; 45 ; 50
24. 10 ; 20 ; 30 ; 40 ; 50
25. 10

Activity

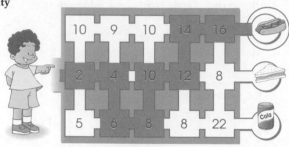

6 More about Addition and Subtraction

1. 5 ; 5 ; 2 ; 2
2. 13 ; 13 ; 9 ; 9
3. 16 ; 16 ; 7 ; 7

4 – 5. (Suggested answers)

4. 4 ; 7 ; 11
   11 ; 4 ; 7
5. 5 ; 6 ; 11
   11 ; 5 ; 6
6. 7
7. 5
8. 7
9. 5
10. 12
11. 15
12. 9
13. 11
14. 8
15. 18
16. 1
17. 8
18. 15
19. 13
20. 16
21. 9
22. 10
23. 12
24. 8
25. 6
26. 8 ; 4 ; 12 ; 12 ;
$$\begin{array}{r} \boxed{8} \\ + \boxed{4} \\ \hline \boxed{1\,2} \end{array}$$
27. 17 ; 8 ; 9 ; 9 ;
$$\begin{array}{r} \boxed{1\,7} \\ - \boxed{8} \\ \hline \boxed{9} \end{array}$$
28. 11 ; 7 ; 4 ; 4 ;
$$\begin{array}{r} \boxed{1\,1} \\ - \boxed{7} \\ \hline \boxed{4} \end{array}$$
29. + ; 13 ;
$$\begin{array}{r} 8 \\ + 5 \\ \hline 1\ 3 \end{array}$$
30. − ; 7 ;
$$\begin{array}{r} 1\ 3 \\ -\ \ 6 \\ \hline 7 \end{array}$$

Activity

1. 4
2. 3
3. 9
4. 10
5. 12
6. 5

7 Money

1. Loonie ; 1
2. Toonie ; 2
3. Quarter ; 25
4. Nickel ; 5
5. Penny ; 1
6. Dime ; 10
7. 4 ; 2 ; 3 ; 2 ; 3 ; 3
8.
9.

ISBN: 978-1-927042-10-6

10.   11.

12.

13.

14.

15.

16. 7   17. 9
18. 8   19. 10
20.

21. 4 ; 2 ; 3 ; 1   22. 9 ; 4 ; 13 ; 13
23. 10 ; 2 ; 8 ; 8

Activity

1. 6   2. 10

Midway Test

1. 2 ; 1 ; 3   2. 1 ; 3 ; 2
3.

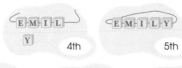

4. 2nd   5. 2
6a. 7 ; Seven   b. 5 ; Five
7.   ; 13   8.   ; 15
9. 7 ; 8 ; 10
10. 29 ; 28 ; 25
11. 77 ; 79 ; 80

12. 40 ; 50 ; 60 ; 10
13. 20 ; 22 ; 24 ; 2
14. 40 ; 45 ; 50 ; 5
15. 8   16. 3
17. 8   18. 14
19. 3 ; 8   20. 57
21. 1   22. 9
23. 9   24. 6
25. 80   26. 6
27. Penny ; 1   28. Loonie ; 1
29. Quarter ; 25   30. Toonie ; 2
31. 15 ; 10 ; 9 ; A
32.
33.
34.

35. 4   36. 2
37. 8   38. 15
39. 8   40. 3
41. 9   42. 12
43. 5   44. 12
45. 4 ; | 1 0 | 46. 13 ; | 7 |
        | − 6 | | + 6 |
        | 4 | | 1 3 |
47. 5 ; | 1 4 |
        | − 9 |
        | 5 |

8   Measurement

1 – 4.

ISBN: 978-1-927042-10-6   Canadian Curriculum MathSmart (Grade 1)   **75**

5. C ; B ; A   6. 6 ; 2

7. 12 ; 4   8. B

9. A   10. C

11. 24   12. 15

13. 16   14.

15. C

16.   17.

18.

19. B   20. C

21.   22.

23.   24.

25.   26. **10**

27.   28.

Activity

9   Shapes

1. ; Circle   ; Rectangle

    ; Triangle   ; Square

2. 2 ; 5 ; 3 ; 2 ; 1 ; 2 ; 1

3. ; Triangle ; 3 ; 3

4. ; Rectangle ; 4 ; 4

5. ; Hexagon ; 6 ; 6

6. ; Pentagon ; 5 ; 5

7 – 9. (Suggested answers)

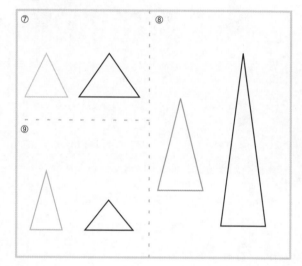

10. Yes   11. Yes

12. No

13.   14.

15.   16.

17.   18.

19.   20.

ISBN: 978-1-927042-10-6

Activity

    8

10 Solids

1.

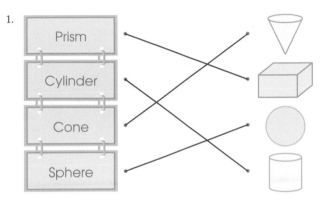

2. Cone : A, G

   Cylinder : B, H

   Prism : D, F

   Sphere : C, E

3.  ; Cylinder

4.  ; Sphere

5.  ; Cone

6.  ; Prism

7. 2 ; 3 ; 5 ; 2

8.

9.

10.

11.

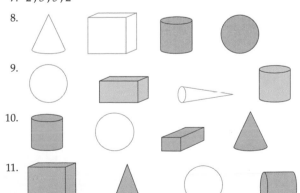

12. Cone ; Cylinder

13. B   14. B

15. C

Activity

    D

11 Directions

1. in front of   2. left

3. inside   4. over

5. behind   6. outside

7. right   8. left

9. under   10. inside

11. over   12. in front of

13. behind   14. outside

15 – 17.

18. B   19. C

20 – 24. (Suggested answers)

20. Pat is inside the box.

21. Annie is under the tree.

22. Michael is jumping over Tim.

23. Jack is behind Pat.

24. Tim is under Michael.

Activity

1. inside   2. left

12 Time

1. Fall ; Summer ; Winter ; Spring

2. 4 ; 1 ; 2 ; 3   3. Monday

4. Thursday   5. Tuesday

6. Thursday   7. Sunday

8. Saturday   9. 7

10. 3   11. 9:00 or 9 o'clock

12. 6:30   13. 5:00 or 5 o'clock

14. 7:30

15. 12:00 or 12 o'clock

16. 6:00 or 6 o'clock

17. 1:30

18. nearly 1:00

19. nearly 3:30

20. A: B:

C :

Activity

13 Patterning

1. 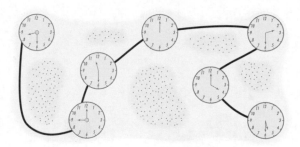   2.

3.   4.

5.   6.

7.

8a.

b. No

9a.

b. Yes

10.

11.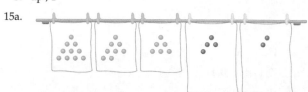

12.

13.

14a.

b. up ; 1

15a.

b. down ; 2

16. (Suggested answer)

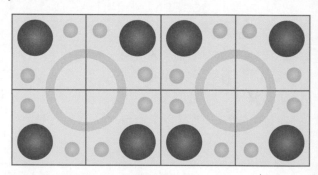

17. 14 ; 16 ; 18 ; +2 each time

18. 35 ; 40 ; 45 ; +5 each time

19. 60 ; 70 ; 80 ; +10 each time

Activity

14 Graphs and Probability

1. 3   2.

3.   4. 4

5.   6. 2

7. 16

ISBN: 978-1-927042-10-6

8.

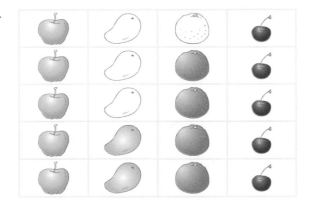

9. 4
10. 7
11. 3
12. 16
13. 4
14. No
15. Yes
16. No
17. Yes
18. Yes
19. No
20. No
21. Yes

22. sometimes ; never ; often

23a. often ; sometimes ; never

b. sometimes ; never ; often

Activity

(Suggested answer)

Final Test

1. shorter ; 5
2. B ; 25
3. B
4.
5. Triangle ; 3 ; 3
6. Pentagon ; 5 ; 5
7. Rectangle ; 4 ; 4
8. Hexagon ; 6 ; 6
9.
10.
11.
12.
13. Cone
14. Prism
15. Sphere
16. Cylinder
17. flat faces
18. be stacked up
19. roll, slide
20. over

21. behind
22. left
23. inside
24a. 13
b. 5
25a. 7
b. 14
26. Fall
27. Winter
28. Spring
29. Summer

30.

31.

32. 7
33. 39
34. 36
35. 45
36. 80
37. 20

38.  ; 4:30

39.  ; 5:30

40. 8
41. 11
42. 6
43. 8
44. 12
45. 2
46. 10

47a. often   b. never   c. sometimes

48.

49. 11

ISBN: 978-1-927042-10-6